Animal Show and Tell

# Animals in the Jungle

Élisabeth de Lambilly-Bresson

 **Gareth Stevens**
Publishing

# The Zebra

I am a zebra.
I have stripes,
black and white,
from my head to my hooves.
I am a wild horse,
and I gallop
as fast as the wind.

# The Lion

I am a lion.
Look at my bushy mane!
It circles my head
like a wreath.
I am a fierce hunter
with a loud and scary roar.
I am the king of the jungle.

# The Crocodile

I am a crocodile.
I look like a giant lizard.
I am a strong swimmer,
but, sometimes, I just float
like a log in the water.
I have many sharp teeth.
Maybe that is why
animals run away from me!

# The Hippopotamus

I am a hippopotamus.
My body is heavy
and shaped like a barrel.
I swim well in rivers,
and I love to take mud baths!

# The Elephant

I am an elephant.
I am gray.  I am big,
the biggest on land!
I use my long trunk
the way you use your hand.
My big ears hear well
and flap like huge fans.

# The Giraffe

I am a giraffe.
With my long legs,
and even longer neck,
I am the tallest animal
in the jungle.
I am so tall
I can nibble treetops.

# The Monkey

I am a monkey.
My body swings and swoops
with ease.
I love to eat
sweet fruit and leaves,
and that is why I live in trees.

**Please visit our Web site at: www.garethstevens.com**
**For a free color catalog describing Gareth Stevens Publishing's**
**list of high-quality books, call 1-800-542-2595 (USA) or**
**1-800-387-3178 (Canada).**

**Library of Congress Cataloging-in-Publication Data**

Lambilly-Bresson, Elisabeth de.
   [Dans la jungle. English]
   Animals in the jungle / Elisabeth de Lambilly-Bresson. — North American ed.
      p. cm. — (Animal show and tell)
   ISBN: 978-0-8368-8206-3 (lib. bdg.)
   1. Jungle animals—Juvenile literature. I. Title.
  QL112.L3413   2007
  591.734—dc22                           2007002554

This North American edition first published in 2008 by
**Gareth Stevens Publishing**
A Weekly Reader® Company
1 Reader's Digest Road
Pleasantville, NY 10570-7000 USA

Translation: Gini Holland
Gareth Stevens editor: Gini Holland
Gareth Stevens art direction and design: Tammy West

This edition copyright © 2008 by Gareth Stevens, Inc. Original edition copyright
© 2001 by Mango Jeunesse Press. First published as *Les animinis: Dans la jungle*
by Mango Jeunesse Press.

Printed in the United States of America

1 2 3 4 5 6 7 8 9 11 10 09 08 07